# The Museum of Scotland

We hope that you will make yourself at home in Scotland's treasure house, the place of real things found, made and used in Scotland. It is also a place where you will meet many of the people of Scotland's past.

The Museum of Scotland displays a unique collection of material that helps to explain the land and its people. Here you will find rocks that shaped the country's landscape, evidence of the earliest wildlife, artefacts shedding light on prehistory, and objects opening doors to our historic past.

This large building displays over ten thousand objects on six levels. The purpose of this guide is to explain how the material is arranged and to help you find your way around. It is also a souvenir of your visit, a reminder of what you have seen and what will be waiting for you when you return - as we hope you will.

The Museum is divided into seven main sections:

**LEVEL 0**
✤ Beginnings: landscape and wildlife before the first farmers

**LEVEL 0**
✤ Early People: from about 8000 BC to about AD 1100

**LEVELS 1 & 2**
✤ The Kingdom of the Scots: about 900 to 1707

**LEVEL 3**
✤ Scotland Transformed: 1707 to the 19th century

✤ **Discovery Centre**

**LEVELS 4 & 5**
✤ Industry and Empire: the 19th century to 1914

**LEVEL 6**
✤ Twentieth Century

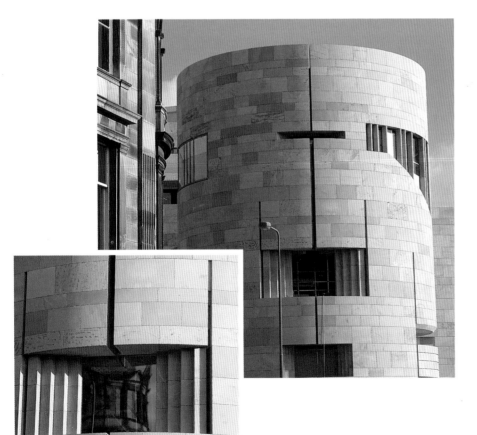

# Make the most of your visit

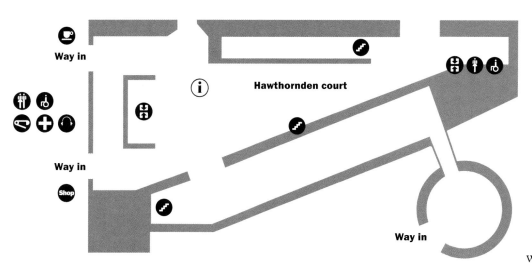

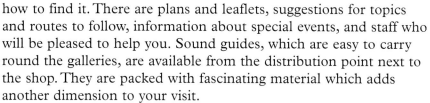

Do you have a particular interest? Just half an hour to spare? Are you on a group visit? Or a day out with the family? Are you hoping for a lecture or a film? Or just a quiet browse?

Whatever you have in mind, the best place to start is in the Hawthornden Court on Level 1, where you will find information about what is on display and how to find it. There are plans and leaflets, suggestions for topics and routes to follow, information about special events, and staff who will be pleased to help you. Sound guides, which are easy to carry round the galleries, are available from the distribution point next to the shop. They are packed with fascinating material which adds another dimension to your visit.

In addition to the exhibition galleries, there are a lecture theatre (the Dunfermline Room), cinema, restaurant and shop.

In the galleries themselves, look out for the labels written by members of the NMS Junior Board - written by children, enjoyed by everyone! - and Discovery Points, which investigate selected objects in detail. The Discovery Centre on Level 3 is a hands-on investigation centre designed for children and families, but unaccompanied adults are also welcome.

On Level 1 the ExhibIT room is equipped with computers where visitors can access SCRAN (Scottish Cultural Resources Access Network) which provides information on museum, gallery and archive collections throughout Scotland. You can also use a number of interactive screen presentations on themes related to Museum of Scotland displays. This facility enables you to explore beyond the material on display in the Museum of Scotland.

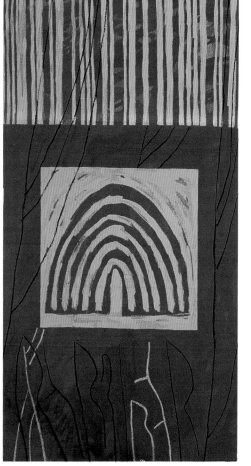

*Tapestry designed by Kate Whiteford, hand woven by the Edinburgh Tapestry Company. The tapestry is displayed near the tower entrance to the Museum of Scotland.*

# Beginnings

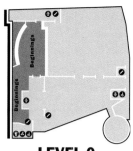

The Museum of Scotland begins with the story of Scotland's landscape and wildlife. You will find *Beginnings* at the east end of Level 0.

The first part of *Beginnings* shows how the piece of land we now call Scotland journeyed over the earth's surface and changed dramatically in shape, landscape and climate. The story is told through the evidence that is found in the rocks. These changes happened hundreds of millions of years before the first people arrived, but the resulting landscape influenced the wildlife and the human history that followed.

The second part explores the history of Scotland's wildlife after the last Ice Age. It is a story of change, survival and extinction.

An evidence trail shows how we can interpret the evidence of the present in order to recreate the past. There are specimens that can be touched. Specially commissioned paintings, models of extinct animals, dioramas and audio-visual programmes vividly illustrate Scotland's earliest history.

**History of the Wildlife**

**Beginnings**

*Dyke of black basalt in white marble, Isle of Skye.*

*Arkle and Loch Stack, Sutherland.*

*Great Auk, which became extinct in the 19th century.*

*Fossil fish from Dura Den, Fife. They died when their pond dried up 360 million years ago.*

3

**LEVEL 0**

# Beginnings

How did Scotland come to be what and where it is? The story begins with **The building blocks of Scotland** which shows how rocks trap clues to the environment at the time they are formed. Scotland's known history starts 3400 million years ago, when the oldest Lewisian Gneiss rocks were formed.

The exhibition then focuses on the last 650 million years of Scotland's story. **Icebergs in southern seas** shows Scotland under an iceberg-laden sea. Over geological time, the continents moved over the surface of the earth, joining together and breaking up. What is now Scotland has moved from near the South Pole northwards to where it is today.

The Iapetus Ocean existed between the continents of which Scotland and England were parts. As time passed and the continents on either side moved closer, the ocean grew smaller and smaller. **The Vanishing Ocean** shows how mud from this ocean was squeezed up into the Border Hills, while **Crumpling Scotland** shows how this collision with England and Wales also threw up the Caledonian Mountains, whose eroded remains are today's Highlands.

Scotland carried on to and past the equator, and the rocks and fossils displayed reflect the changing climate and landscapes. **Early land and lake life** presents underwater dioramas of Devonian times, showing freshwater fishes whose fossils are one of Scotland's glories.

*Graptolites in the Iapetus Ocean 435 million years ago.* John Sibbick

*Lewisian Gneiss at Rubh 'Aird-mhicheil, South Uist.*

4

**Volcanoes and tropical seas** takes you to Carboniferous times, around 340 million years ago, when corals lived in the coastal seas and central Scotland was dominated by volcanoes. From the Museum's roof you can see several of these volcanoes, including Edinburgh Castle Rock and Arthur's Seat. One of Scotland's most famous fossils, found at East Kirkton in West Lothian, is *Westlothiana*, often called 'Lizzie'. It may be the earliest known reptile and, if so, close to our ancestry.

Volcanic lava produces fertile soil. Other important legacies of Scotland's ancient landscape are coal and oil. Their origins are explored in the displays on **Tropical coal forests** and, further on, **The high lava plateaus**.

*Arthur's Seat, Edinburgh.*

*Volcanoes and fissure eruptions on the high lava plateau of western Scotland, 60 million years ago.* John Sibbick

**LEVEL 0**

Few creatures lived in **The great Scottish desert** of 260 million years ago, but one we know of is the now extinct dicynodont. In Jurassic times the sea flooded much of the land, as the North Sea and the Atlantic Ocean began to form. In **The new seas** swam ammonites, squid-like belemnites and plesiosaurs, while dinosaurs roamed the land.

The geological displays finish with **The Ice Ages**, which ended only a few thousand years ago. The landscape we know today was scraped and gouged by the huge glaciers that covered much of Scotland. But of course that's not the end of the story. Thanks to erosion, Scotland's landscape is still changing.

*Ammonites, shellfish that once swam in Jurassic seas.*
*A dicynodont in life.* John Sibbick
*Footprints left in the sand by a dicynodont, about 260 million years ago.*

**History of the Wildlife**
continues directly after
**The Ice Ages.**

6

# History of the Wildlife

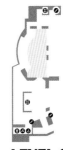

The history of the wildlife relating to the landscape as we now know it began about 11,750 years ago. When the climate began to warm up after the last Icc Age, life returned. **History of the Wildlife** explores some of the consequences, and looks at how human activity has affected the landscape and the life it sustains. Many of the species that flourished after the ice melted have disappeared, but now more efforts are being made to halt the process of extinction and to restore habitats. Today about 20% of Scotland's land area is protected in order to preserve habitats and their plants and animals.

**Investigating change** looks at the evidence for change and allows us to reconstruct past habitats. Four topics demonstrate what we can learn from these different kinds of evidence. **Relict species** looks at Arctic species found in Scotland, which tell us that once the climate was much colder than it is now. **Fossils** provide evidence of plants and animals that are now extinct. **Radiocarbon dating** explains how scientists can tell when a particular species existed and when environmental changes took place. **Pollen analysis** helps us to understand what plants flourished where, and provides clues as to what past habitats were like.

*Fossil skull of Beaver from the Borders, now extinct.*

*Capercaillie, reintroduced to Scotland in 1837.*

*Polar Campion (left) and Arctic Poppy, Arctic plants known in Scotland from fossil seeds, but now extinct.*

7

**LEVEL 0**

The history of the forests examines one type of environment. Fossil evidence tells of the reindeer and the lemmings of the Arctic tundra of the last Ice Age. A diorama shows how the tundra was replaced by oak forests in the Lowlands and Scots pine in the Highlands: little natural forest survives, largely because of the activities of farmers over nearly 6000 years. Many large species, such as the brown bear and the lynx, disappeared and new ones, mainly small, were introduced by people. Some extinctions resulted from climate change, others were brought about by human activity.

**The biodiversity and habitats of Scotland** explores the great variety of species and habitats. Scotland's seas and 12,000 kilometres (7500 miles) of coastline provide varying habitats which are home to almost 40,000 species of animal, plant and micro-organism. You can find out about some of them in **Seas and shores**.

Scotland's 30,000 lochs and 6600 river systems hold 90% of Britain's freshwater, and there are also marshes and peat bogs. **Freshwater and wetlands** explores these habitats. **Mountain and moorland** focuses on two other characteristic Scottish habitats - mountains have been the least affected by human activity. But most of Scotland - 78% - consists of human-made habitats. In **Urban and farmland habitats** you can find out about the impact this has had on wildlife.

As you come out of **History of the Wildlife** the entrance to *Early People* is on your left, directly opposite the main lifts.

*Skull of Aurochs or Wild Ox from the Borders - extinct in the Iron Age.*

*The Lynx became extinct due to habitat loss and hunting.*

*Mountain Hare, a relict species from the Highlands introduced to the Borders and islands.*

8

# Early People

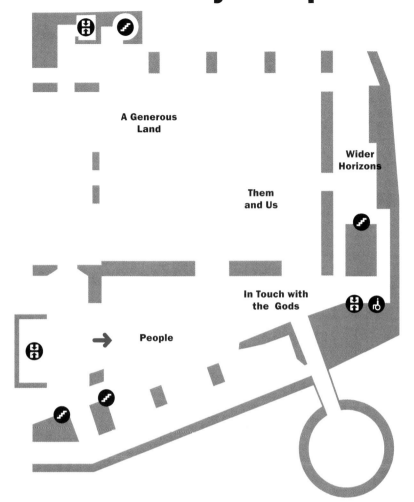

A Generous
Land

Wider
Horizons

Them
and Us

In Touch with
the Gods

People

As the climate warmed after the Ice Age, people
followed the animals into a land that provided the
resources they needed in order to thrive. It was the
beginning of humanity's 10,000 years of living in Scotland.

*Early People* explores how people lived, from around 8000
BC to AD 1100. What did people eat? How did they
protect themselves from the elements? What resources were
available to them and how did they use them? How much
contact did they have with other people in other places?
What sort of spiritual life did they have?

These are some of the questions tackled in the exhibition's four main
sections, which include 23 different themes. Each display is
numbered.

*Hunting scene from the carved stone
from Hilton of Cadboll, Ross and
Cromarty, AD 700-800.*

*Silver panther-shaped handles of a
Roman wine container, from a hoard
of Roman silver found at Traprain
Law, East Lothian, about AD 400.*

*Gold collar from Auchentaggart,
Dumfriesshire, about 2000 BC.*

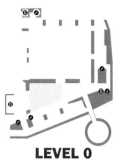

**LEVEL 0**

# People

Who were the people of prehistory? In most cases we don't know. We don't know what they looked like, how they dressed or did their hair, what they thought or how they spoke. But we do know that every object displayed here has some connection with an individual or a group of people. Someone made it, someone wore it, someone used it. Many of the things you will see were found in someone's home or someone's grave.

*People* introduces the exhibition's absentees, through figures sculpted by Sir Eduardo Paolozzi. The figures stand for Scotland's early people. They are abstract because there is little evidence to help us identify and describe them realistically. Each group of figures also highlights a section of the exhibition. *A Generous Land* looks at the land's resources and how people used them. *Wider Horizons* explores the theme of contact with a wider world and the movement of people, goods and ideas. In *Them and Us* issues of conflict and imperialism, power and status, are examined, while *In Touch with the Gods* concentrates on spiritual life.

The displays are arranged to take you on a journey through these themes, and you can choose what interests you as you go. Each case includes a map and a timeline, to help you locate where the objects were found and their approximate date.

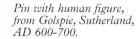

*Pin with human figure, from Golspie, Sutherland, AD 600-700.*

*Roman marble head from Hawkshaw, Peeblesshire, about AD 100.*

*Hinged collar from Stitchill, Roxburghshire, about AD 100.*

To begin your journey, turn left as you face the monumental stone from Hilton of Cadboll and enter *A Generous Land.*

10

# A Generous Land

The first thing you see as you enter this gallery is a tenth-century Pictish carved stone from Bullion in Angus, showing a warrior on horseback enjoying a tipple from his drinking horn. This introduces the themes of food and drink and also agriculture, hunting and gathering, beginning with **Fat of the land** (Displays B1-9). The utensils used to prepare and eat food not only tell us about what people ate, but also show how eating could be a social event, where display and fine objects mattered as well as fine food. How and what you ate was often a way of defining status.

How did Scotland's early people acquire the food they needed? **Tilling the soil, tending the beasts** (Displays C1-6) looks at farming which was an important means of producing food from around 4000 BC. Crops were grown and cattle, sheep and pigs were raised, which provided much more than food. **Fruits of the wild** (Displays D1-8) is about how food was collected from the wild, by gathering, hunting and fishing. For the first four millennia of human presence these were the only ways of obtaining food. Surviving equipment - bows and arrows, spears, harpoons, fishing gear - tells us something about the techniques used, and also that hunting continued as a sporting activity after it was no longer vital for survival.

*Sculptured stone from Bullion, Angus.*

*Grave group from Crawford, Lanarkshire.*

*Scratched drawing of dogs chasing a deer, St Blane's, Bute, Argyll, AD 600-1000.*

11

**LEVEL 0**

Scotland's early inhabitants were highly skilled in their use of the land's abundant resources. Bone and antler (Displays E1-6) were versatile and widely used - the plastic of prehistory. Skins and woven textiles (Displays F1-4 and G1-4) provided clothes, shoes, horse trappings. Although the textiles themselves generally don't survive - look out for the hood from Orkney, a rare exception - spindle whorls and parts of looms tell us that weaving was important.

Each display in this area looks at how objects were made, what raw materials and tools were used and the skills required to use them. Woodworkers, for example, used axes, adzes, mallets, wedges, knives, chisels, gouges and drills to take them from felling a tree to a finished object (Displays H1-10). The Romans had professional carpenters with a fully specialized toolkit, including saws, hammers and different types of nail.

Stone was a versatile material used to make a variety of objects, from tools and weapons to jewellery, as well as for buildings and monuments. The displays in **Shaping stone** (Displays J1-6) include three case studies on stone which was quarried or mined. Other displays illustrate the tools and skills of the mason.

*Woven woollen hood, St Andrew's Parish, Orkney, about AD 260-615.*

*Leatherworker's toolbox from Evie, Orkney, AD 640-860.*

*Wooden keg, Morvern, Argyll, AD 120-324.*

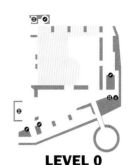
Pottery making (Displays K1-6) came to Scotland at the same time as farming. Clay could be shaped into vessels using simple technology. The potter's wheel was used by the Romans.

**Melting rocks, forging metal**
(Displays L1-8) explores the techniques of working the metals available, from copper and lead to iron and gold. Metal transformed the lives of early people. It allowed them to produce more effective tools and weapons, and delicate and prestigious jewellery. Bronze, a mixture of copper and tin, was in use in Scotland by about 2500 BC. It was relatively easy to work by hammering or melting and casting. When iron working was introduced in Scotland, around 700 BC, new skills, those of the blacksmith, had to be learnt. Silver was worked from metals brought in from outwith Scotland, though native gold was used.

**Broken glass** (Displays M1-4) shows how imported glass was melted down and recycled into beads and ornaments, and includes examples of faience, an earlier glass-like material, which was made in Scotland.

Many of these skills were utilized in the construction, furnishing, heating and lighting of homes and other buildings. This is illustrated in **About the house**, the final part of *A Generous Land* (Displays N1-4). This area includes a screen programme which looks at the range of materials and techniques used in building and the effects this activity had on the Scottish landscape.

*Crescent-shaped bronze strip from Balmaclellan, Kirkcudbrightshire, about AD 100.*

*Roman glass jug from Turriff, Aberdeenshire, about AD 100.*

*Decorated base of a fancy pot from Kilmartin, Argyll, 3500-2800 BC.*

At the end of
**About the house**
continue into the
west gallery for the
beginning of *Wider
Horizons.*

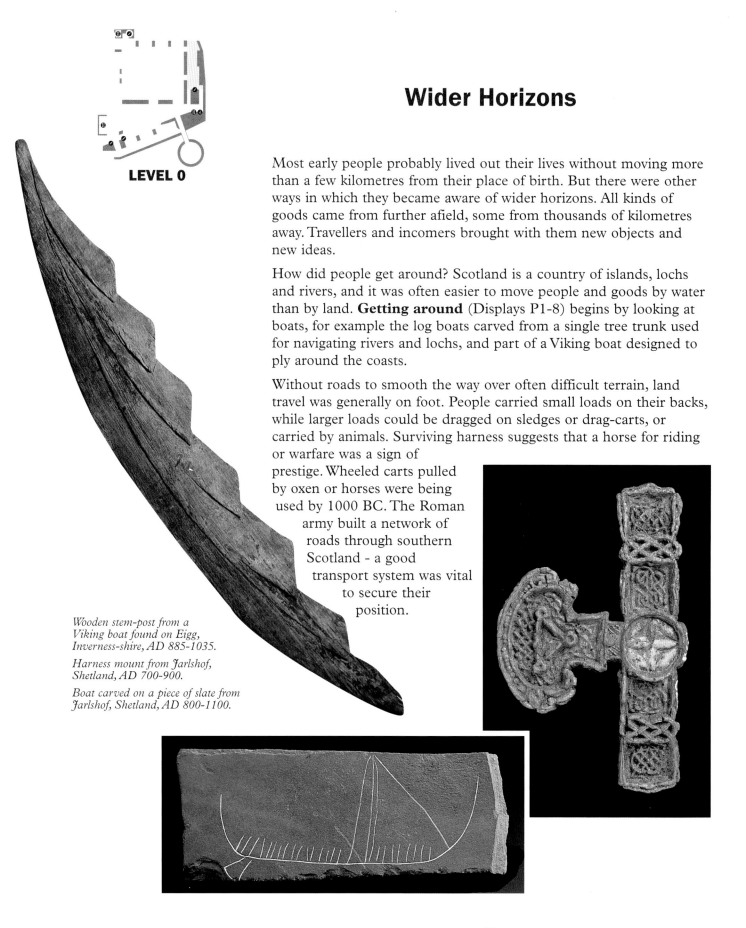

# Wider Horizons

Most early people probably lived out their lives without moving more than a few kilometres from their place of birth. But there were other ways in which they became aware of wider horizons. All kinds of goods came from further afield, some from thousands of kilometres away. Travellers and incomers brought with them new objects and new ideas.

How did people get around? Scotland is a country of islands, lochs and rivers, and it was often easier to move people and goods by water than by land. **Getting around** (Displays P1-8) begins by looking at boats, for example the log boats carved from a single tree trunk used for navigating rivers and lochs, and part of a Viking boat designed to ply around the coasts.

Without roads to smooth the way over often difficult terrain, land travel was generally on foot. People carried small loads on their backs, while larger loads could be dragged on sledges or drag-carts, or carried by animals. Surviving harness suggests that a horse for riding or warfare was a sign of prestige. Wheeled carts pulled by oxen or horses were being used by 1000 BC. The Roman army built a network of roads through southern Scotland - a good transport system was vital to secure their position.

*Wooden stem-post from a Viking boat found on Eigg, Inverness-shire, AD 885-1035.*

*Harness mount from Jarlshof, Shetland, AD 700-900.*

*Boat carved on a piece of slate from Jarlshof, Shetland, AD 800-1100.*

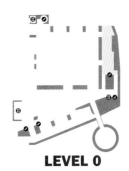

**Moving things, travelling people** shows how objects, ideas and people moved around the country, and often came to Scotland over great distances (Displays Q1-18). Objects moved from place to place within Scotland, some exchanged, some as gifts or booty. Both raw materials and finished products came into Scotland from outside. The hoard from Balmashanner (Display Q2) shows a mix of things with origins in northern and central Europe, England, Ireland and Scotland. It illustrates the extent of movement and contact.

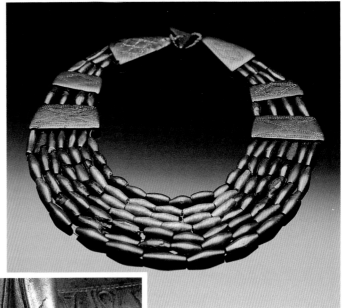

There were links with England and with the continent of Europe. Many objects illustrate the strong contacts between communities in the west of Scotland and Ireland. Objects from distant parts were sometimes copied by native craftworkers, which helped to spread new ideas and ways of doing things. Viking settlement from the ninth century AD brought in Scandinavian items and linked Scotland with an extensive trading network which reached as far as the Black Sea and Baghdad (Displays Q8-13).

The Romans, a presence in Scotland 700 years earlier, brought with them a highly organized supply system (Displays Q14-18). This supported the Roman army, bringing in goods from other parts of the empire, as well as making locally what the soldiers needed.

*Necklace made from Whitby jet and cannel coal, found at Poltalloch, Argyll, 2300-1800 BC.*

*Detail of a Mediterranean wine jug from the Roman camp at Newstead, Roxburghshire, AD 80-100.*

*Silver coin (dirham) from Baghdad, AD 945-6, part of the hoard found at Skaill in Orkney.*

Turn left into the parallel gallery to find *Them and Us.*

# Them and Us

Powerful images of warriors on three sculpted stones introduce **Bloodshed, weapons and heroes** (Displays R1-18), the first part of *Them and Us*. A 5500-year-old arrowhead lodged in a human vertebra

is the oldest evidence we have of possible hostilities in Scotland, followed by weapons and accessories of war relating to several thousand years of conflict. But warfare was on a small scale, concerned with raiding rather than territorial conquest. A highlight is the extraordinary carnyx, or war trumpet, used ceremonially as well as to inspire warriors and terrify the enemy.

Courage and success on the battlefield brought rewards and impressive weapons signalled a warrior's status. This is vividly demonstrated by the Vikings (Display R10). At first a feared enemy, they took over territory in order to settle, and became a permanent part of life and culture, particularly in Shetland, Orkney and the Hebrides.

The Roman army came north into Scotland in AD 80 (Displays R11-18). No one in Scotland had encountered organization and technology like it. The Roman army's

highly disciplined and well-equipped legions and auxiliaries were supported by an elaborate supply system and an impressive medical service. Among the most striking Roman objects displayed are the parade helmets worn by cavalrymen during tournaments, and a horse's parade harness (Displays R17-18).

*War trumpet or carnyx found at Deskford, Banffshire, AD 100-200.*

*Spear-carrying warriors on a carved stone from Brough of Birsay, Orkney, AD 700-800.*

*Face-masks which formed part of parade helmets worn by Roman soldiers, Newstead, AD 80-100.*

The Roman army occupied lowland Scotland three times. During these periods, in total fifty years, the Romans could be hard masters. But in spite of their power they only occupied lowland Scotland, with little impact north of the Rivers Forth and Clyde. In the second century AD they built the Antonine Wall to divide Roman Scotland from the area further north.

**Roman invaders** (Displays S1-15) shows relations between the Romans and the native population. An array of Roman coins illustrates Roman campaigns, but the native way of life was not much affected by the Roman presence. Most people had little contact with the invaders. Material displayed illustrates the Roman strategy of keeping the peace through diplomatic contacts with important native chiefs, to whom they gave gifts. The natives valued Roman objects, but often for reasons which had little to do with their original purpose (Displays S7-10).

The treasure from Traprain Law in East Lothian is spectacular evidence of Roman influence even after they had left Scotland (Displays S13-15). It was probably given to a native chief to secure his loyalty at a time when Roman Britain was collapsing and the legions were preparing to abandon the province.

*Part of the silver treasure from Traprain Law, East Lothian, about AD 400.*

*A victorious Roman soldier, from a slab on the Antonine Wall at Bridgeness, West Lothian, about AD 140.*

*Roman bowls from a hoard found at Helmsdale, Sutherland, about AD 200-300.*

**Letters of authority** is about the power of literacy (Displays T1-7). Writing was brought to Scotland by the Romans, and Latin inscriptions on stones and coins are part of its legacy. Reading and writing were essential to the control and administration of a complex empire. Most Roman soldiers had some ability to read and write, and marked their belongings, but the native people had never been literate. They depended on an oral tradition for knowledge of history, culture and law, transmitting information by word of mouth.

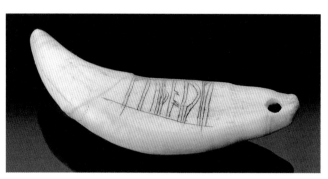

*Seal's tooth amulet inscribed with runes, Brough of Birsay, AD 850-1200.*

*Inscription from a slab on the Antonine Wall at Bridgeness, West Lothian, AD 142-3.*

Literacy left with the Romans, to return in the fifth century AD with the arrival of Christianity, which brought with it Latin as the language of the Church. Two other systems of writing came into use in Scotland: ogham which conveyed the Celtic languages, and runes which represented the Germanic languages of the Anglians and Vikings. All these methods of writing were the province of the aristocracy. As with the Romans, written inscriptions such as that on the Bressay stone were used to impress and convey superior status. Most people were still illiterate, and many regarded writing as a form of magic - the seal's tooth, with the first six letters of the runic alphabet, is an amulet.

**Symbols of power** explores how rare and precious materials, sophisticated craftwork and conspicuous consumption signal power and status (Displays V1-7). This is demonstrated through jewellery, and decorated implements and weapons. The eighth-century Hunterston brooch found in Ayrshire is an outstanding example of an artefact created to impress. The production of such magnificent objects was carefully controlled by those in power. For example, at Dunadd in modern Argyll, the capital of Dál Riata, elaborate objects were made. From this centre of power gifts were presented to lesser chiefs to ensure their loyalty. Great feasts were another form of conspicuous consumption and status symbol.

**Burying treasure, sacrificing wealth** shows how valued objects were buried for a number of reasons (Displays U1-5). The Skaill hoard of Viking silver was probably buried for safekeeping. Other hoards were clearly offerings to the gods. The hoard from Carlingwark was placed in a huge cauldron and thrown into a loch - it was never meant to be recovered (Display U3). Hoards of valuable objects were deposited to impress not just the gods but also the community who witnessed these demonstrations of wealth, power and generosity. They could include weapons and tools as well as jewellery and precious metals.

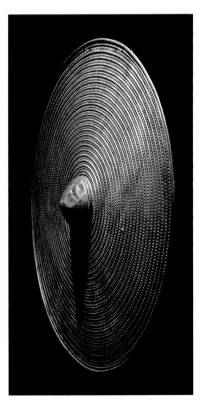

*Richly decorated brooch found at Hunterston, Ayrshire, AD 800.*

*Silver chain with decoration, Whitecleugh, Lanark, AD 500-600.*

*Bronze ceremonial shield found at Yetholm, Roxburghshire, 1150-750 BC.*

*Maceheads from Airdens, Sutherland and Urquhart, Moray, 3100-2800 BC.*

As you leave this part of the gallery you will see directly in front of you the start of the next theme, *In Touch with the Gods.*

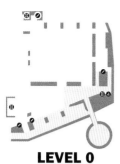

# In Touch with the Gods

The final section of *Early People* is about ways of trying to make sense of life and death and belief in the supernatural. **Dead and sometimes buried** shows how people dealt with death in early Scotland (Displays W1-21).

Burial practices varied, and there are some periods for which we have no evidence at all. The earliest formal burials we know of are those of the early farmers, who often buried their dead in communal tombs. From around 2500 BC individual burials became common. Then, around 1700 BC, cremation was favoured. The Romans brought their own traditions, including the use of elaborate grave monuments for high-ranking officials.

With Christianity came burials without grave goods in graves aligned east-west, to ensure that on Judgement Day the dead could rise to face their maker (Display W6). Viking settlers in the ninth century AD brought another set of pagan practices, with people buried fully clothed with their possessions, some even buried in their boats.

The disposal of the dead was an important social ritual which often highlighted aspects of the deceased's identity (Display W10). Death was regarded as a crossing of the threshold from the world of the living to the world of the ancestors and gods. For Scotland's earliest people this meant leaving bodies on rubbish heaps to return to nature. Later, parts of bodies were used in symbolic rituals.

*Sculpture of a lioness and her prey, found at Cramond, near Edinburgh, AD 140-250.*

*Decorated lintel stone from a passage tomb, Eday, Orkney, 3100-2500 BC.*

*Grave goods from Culduthel, near Inverness, 2300-1800 BC.*

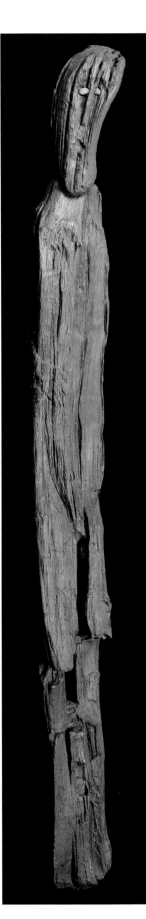

Follow the passage, which continues the exploration of the treatment of the dead, to the tower where you will find **Glimpses of the sacred** (Displays X1-11). We have only a fragmented notion of early beliefs and religious practices, but the material assembled here illustrates how strong a part was played in everyday life by belief in the supernatural. We can recognize that many objects have spiritual significance, although we often don't know exactly what it is.

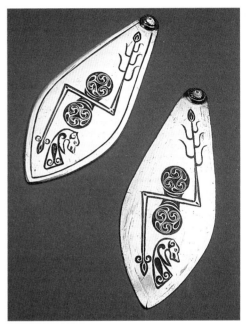

One of the most intriguing objects is the figure found in Ballachulish, probably representing a goddess. The stone balls carved with motifs are also enigmatic, but probably had a ceremonial function. Offerings to the gods marked important events in a family or community - objects were often buried in the foundations of a house, for example. We know little about the ceremonies which must have accompanied these occasions, but feasting, using special vessels and equipment, probably played a part.

The central area of this display presents Pictish engravings on stones and small objects. These symbols have attracted attention and speculation for centuries but no one knows exactly what their meaning is. Even without that understanding, we can recognize their power and the existence of a complex belief system.

*Figure from Ballachulish, Inverness-shire, 730-520 BC.*

*Plaques with Pictish decoration found at Norrie's Law, Fife, AD 600-700.*

*Carved stone ball from Towie, Aberdeenshire, about 2500 BC.*

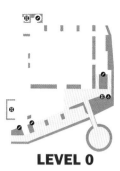

**LEVEL 0**

Only with written information can we get a better understanding of religious beliefs and practices. This applies to Roman religion and early Christianity, the subject of **Gods of the frontier, God of the Book**. For the Romans (Displays Y1-27) there was an empire-wide state religion, centred on the emperor, Jupiter, Juno and Minerva, but allowing scope for groups and individuals to worship the gods of their choice. These could include the gods of conquered tribes, such as Brigantia, a local goddess adopted by some soldiers.

Christianity came to Scotland gradually, spreading from other parts of Europe (Displays Y13-27). The Galloway church associated with St Ninian and Whithorn made the first impact. Further north, a wealth of evidence from the western mainland and islands shows that this was fertile territory for Christian missionaries from Ireland, such as St Columba. The Anglian church affected mainly the southeast, while the Pictish areas to the north and east were influenced from both the west and the south.

Christianity's hold on Scotland was strengthened as local rulers were converted. The treasure from St Ninian's Isle is a fine example of material showing Christian symbolism on aristocratic possessions. But images carved on the stone cross from Papil indicate that echoes of older beliefs lingered well after the arrival of the new religion.

*Carved stone from Papil, Shetland, AD 700-900.*

*Detail from a bowl, part of the treasure found on St Ninian's Isle, Shetland, AD 720-850.*

*Statue of Brigantia from Birrens, Dumfriesshire, AD 120-180.*

To continue on to *The Kingdom of the Scots* go upstairs to Level 1. The main entrance is from the Hawthornden Court.

# The Kingdom of the Scots

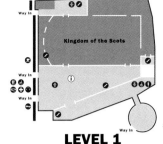

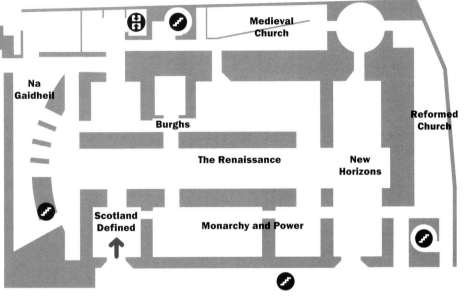

The way in to *The Kingdom of the Scots* is marked by the Dupplin Cross. Here you are entering Scotland in history, the period where our understanding of objects from the past is aided by written accounts. *The Kingdom of the Scots* takes Scotland from its emergence as a nation to 1707, when the Union of the Scottish and English parliaments set the scene for the centuries to follow.

It explores the Gaelic heritage, the impact of Christianity and the emergence of a strong monarchy. It looks at towns and trade, and illustrates Scotland's position in the wider world. Scottish merchants, scholars and soldiers travelled all over Europe.

You will find evidence of a vibrant nation and an inventive people, but also of political and religious conflict. Scotland played its part in both the great artistic flowering of the Renaissance and the far-reaching changes of the Reformation. All of this is explored in eight themes, beginning with *Scotland Defined*.

The Village Dance *or* Lowland Wedding, *after de Witt.*

*Pistol made in Dundee by Robert Alison, 1618.*

*Gold lion noble of James VI.*

*Cross from Dupplin, Perthshire, 9th century.*

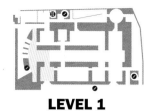

# Scotland Defined
## Land and people become a kingdom

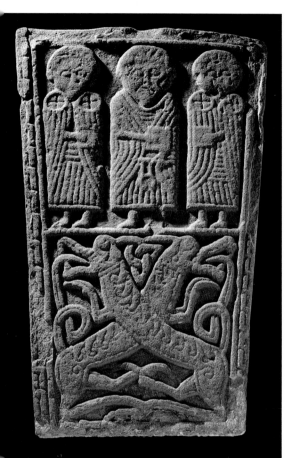

*Scotland Defined* introduces all the galleries concerned with Scotland's historic past. It displays objects which illustrate the emerging Scottish nation and the different peoples who became a part of it.

Near the sandstone cross-slab from Invergowrie in Angus, evidence of both Christian and pre-Christian Scotland, is the tiny Monymusk reliquary (Case 1). Also known as the *Brec Bennoch* (Gaelic for Speckled Peaked One), it is one of the Museum's most important objects. Probably dating from the eighth century, it is linked with St Columba, a key figure in the spread of Christianity in Scotland, and with Robert the Bruce, the hero king who defeated an English army at the battle of Bannockburn in 1314.

The walls on either side show two short extracts from the *Declaration of Arbroath* of 1320 which proclaimed the Scots' commitment to independence. You will also find names of kings taken from a king list of the AD 840s. It reminds us of the long tradition of kingship in Scotland.

Pass under the stone arch from Forteviot in Perthshire. In front of you is an oak statue of St Andrew, the patron saint of Scotland (Case 2). From about the 13th century St Andrew and his cross, the saltire, have been symbols of the Scottish nation.

*Sandstone slab from Invergowrie, Perthshire, 9th century.*

*Oak carving of St Andrew, about 1500.*

*The Monymusk reliquary, 8th century.*

24

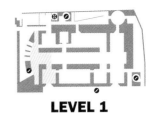

Through to the left, *Scotland Defined* continues with **People**. Here you will find the many different groups of people who had an impact on life and society, language and culture. The Picts (Case 4), the earliest named inhabitants of Scotland, occupied the area north of the Firth of Forth. Although we know little about them they have left their symbols on surviving standing stones. Their language has not survived, except in placenames such as Pitlochry and Pittenweem.

The Britons' Scottish kingdom was Strathclyde, the capital at Dumbarton. The Angles (Case 3) came originally from northern Europe, settling in the Lothians where evidence of their buildings and lifestyle has been found. The Scots, who gave their name to the country, began to cross from Ireland in the fifth century, and 300 years later the Vikings were invading from Scandinavia (Case 5). They left a striking legacy of objects, among the best known of which are the chesspieces which were found in Lewis in the 19th century (Case 6). The last wave of incomers to add significantly to the mix of peoples that populated Scotland were the Anglo-Normans who moved into Scotland in the 12th century (Case 7).

Maps of placenames and surnames help to plot the movement and impact of Scotland's peoples.

*Detail from an Anglian carved stone from Morham, East Lothian.*

*The Lewis chesspieces, 12th century.*

On the left, as you face the curved wall, is the entrance to *Na Gaidheil*, The Gael.

25

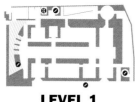

# Na Gaidheil
## The Gael

Those who crossed from Ireland to the west coast of Scotland established a strong Gaelic culture which has since dominated the Western Highlands and Islands. Gaelic became for a time the language of most of Scotland as well as Ireland and has left its imprint on placenames as far south as the Lothians and Galloway.

Displaycd here are objects ranging from the tall stone cross from Eilean Mor, immediately in front of you, to **Highland brooches** (Case 6). They demonstrate the vitality of West Highland art, which was encouraged by the Lords of the Isles who were descended from Somerled, 12th-century King of the Hebrides. The Lordship became particularly powerful in the 14th and 15th centuries.

The Lordship of the Isles had its administrative centre at Finlaggan in Islay. The display on **Finlaggan** (Case 2) shows what can be discovered from the excavation of an ancient site. The excavation was carried out between 1990 and 1997 and has revealed that the Lordship operated from an extensive and well-appointed centre. Evidence of buildings and the way the people there spent their time has been uncovered. Some of it is displayed here along with diagrams and reconstructions which explain the site.

*Highland brooches, 16th and 17th century.*

*Whalebone casket from the West Highlands, 15th-16th century.*

*Highland dirks, 17th-18th century.*

26

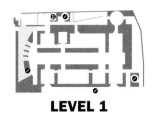
The claymore (Case 3) and images on the sculptured stones are reminders that raiding and warfare were significant features of medieval Highland life. But this is balanced by a vivid culture of poetry, song and decorative art. The clarsach (harp) and the rare Books of Clanranald are striking examples of West Highland art. The *Red Book of Clanranald* is one of the earliest accounts of events in Scotland from a Gaelic viewpoint.

Although the Lordship of the Isles was suppressed by James IV in 1493, West Highland art continued to flourish. You can see this in the characteristic Celtic motifs decorating the later jewellery and weapons displayed in Cases 5 and 6 - and indeed these motifs still survive in modern interpretations of traditional designs.

At the far end of *Na Gaidheil* is an impressive array of firearms and swords from the family armoury of the Lairds of Grant, based in Speyside (Case 8). Intricately-carved powder horns are displayed in Case 7. Beside the armoury hangs a portrait of William Cumming, piper to the Laird of Grant, a well-known image which you can explore in some detail through the Discovery Point.

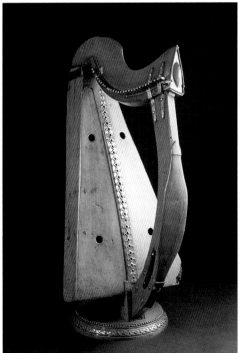

*William Cumming, piper to the Laird of Grant, painted by Richard Waitt in 1714.*

*The Red Book of Clanranald, 17th century.*

*Clarsach, the Lamont harp, about 1500.*

As you leave the Grant piper, we suggest you turn right and retrace your steps until you are again under the painted ceiling from Rossend Castle. The second entrance on the right, under the lintel with the royal arms, takes you into *Monarchy and Power.*

27

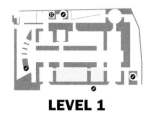

# Monarchy and Power
## The governing of Scotland and the Stewart dynasty

Power in medieval Scotland stemmed from the monarchy. For much of the period Scotland was ruled by the Stewarts, a dynasty of kings and queens who were ambitious, creative and often warlike. Their story begins with Robert the Bruce.

In the first case is a communal drinking cup, the Bute mazer, which was made shortly after the Scottish victory over the English at the battle of Bannockburn in 1314. It features heraldry representing the main supporters of Robert the Bruce, who led the Scots in their fight for independence. There is more on **Robert the Bruce** in Case 3.

The king and the nobility maintained power through the ownership of land, and through the sword. Not surprisingly, there are several weapons and other instruments of violence displayed in *Monarchy and Power*, from the ceremonial sword of the Sempills of Elliestoun (Case 2) and the display on **William Wallace** (Case 3) to the 'Maiden', the Scottish beheading-machine at the far end of the gallery.

Castles also represented power and status. The display on **Threave Castle** (Case 5) tells a story of rivalry between the king and the powerful Douglas family. Another way of signifying power was through wearing gold and silver jewellery. Medieval rings and brooches are displayed in Case 6.

*The Bute mazer, 14th century.*

*Brooch from Kindrochit Castle, Aberdeenshire.*

*The Maiden, a beheading-machine, 16th century.*

28

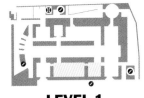

The story of the Stewart monarchs continues in Case 7. But you will find an important part of it in the parallel gallery on *The Renaissance*. The Stewarts fostered the arts, learning and education, as well as alliances with foreign powers, and *The Renaissance* presents some of the results.

*Monarchy and Power* goes on to look at **James VI**, the first monarch to become ruler of both Scotland and England (Cases 9 and 10). He inherited the English throne with the death of Elizabeth I in 1603. James's learning and his determination to control his kingdoms are reflected in the material displayed.

James VI's son and grandson, both called Charles, lived most of their lives in England, but both received a Scottish coronation. They reigned in troubled times. Many Scots were loyal to the Stewarts, others opposed them. Both loyalty and conflict are illustrated in material commemorating Charles I and Charles II (Case 12).

**Law and order** introduces some of the harsher aspects of the State's efforts to maintain control. James VI in particular saw a threat in people, mainly women, accused of witchcraft (Case 15). Political and religious divisions in Scotland continued throughout the 17th century. One of the episodes still recalled is the **Massacre of Glencoe** of 1692, the subject of Case 17.

*Goblet from which James VI is said to have drunk before leaving for London in 1603.*

*Jewellery commemorating Charles I and Charles II.*

**A left turn out of Law and order takes you into the world of the Scottish Renaissance.**

29

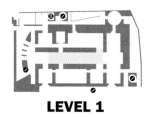

# The Renaissance
## Scotland's contribution to Renaissance art and learning

The Renaissance, a revival in art and learning inspired by classical Greece and Rome, began to influence Scotland in the 15th century. Our display shows how this affected architecture and interior design, jewellery, textiles, metalwork and weapons. Scottish artists and craftsmen combined the new ideas with traditional Scottish designs.

A good place to start is the Cadboll cup in the centre of the gallery (Case 3). This is a striking example of a distinctively Scottish Renaissance style. But look also at the older styles, for example the Gothic panels made for Cardinal Beaton on the south wall.

Mary, Queen of Scots lived in France for many years and, like her father James V and grandfather James IV, represents Renaissance links between France and Scotland. The cast of her tomb - the original is in Westminster Abbey, London - is a dominant feature of the gallery, but look also at the jewellery, coins and medals associated with her in Case 1.

If you finish your exploration of the Renaissance with the cannons at the east end of the gallery, take another look at the painted ceiling from Rossend Castle. This, too, was part of the Scottish Renaissance enthusiasm for colour and decoration.

If you go back to the cannons and turn left through the doorway from Kirkcaldy you will enter *Burghs*. Turn left again and continue until you find yourself in the marketplace of a medieval town.

*Detail from carved wooden panels made for Cardinal Beaton, 1530s.*

*Carved oak medallion thought to represent Margaret Tudor, from Stirling castle, about 1540.*

*Jewellery which belonged to Mary, Queen of Scots, 16th century.*

# Burghs
## Life in Scotland's towns

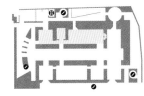
Burghs were Scotland's centres of industry and trade, and also of local government. The first burghs were created by David I in the 12th century. By 1450 there were over 80, mainly in central and eastern Scotland. The original shape and layout of medieval burghs can still be detected in many towns.

The focus of the burgh was the market place, a crowded and busy area where goods and information were exchanged. Like the rest of Europe, Scotland developed as a money economy, and coins are an important aspect of the displays in this area - see Cases 3, 4 and 5 and **The Edinburgh mint** (Case 8).

**Town houses** shows how the signs of successful trade were found in the homes of merchants and manufacturers, many of which contained fine furniture and luxury goods. Although many luxury items, such as glass and Limoges enamels, were imported from abroad, Scottish silversmiths and specialist craftsmen produced high quality work.

In the centre of the main part of this gallery is material from a house in Blyth's Close off Edinburgh's Castlehill. The house has connections with Mary of Guise, the French mother of Mary, Queen of Scots, and a politically influential woman. A Discovery Point explores some aspects of the house and her life.

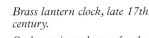

*Brass lantern clock, late 17th century.*

*Seal matrix and press for the burgh of Crail, Fife.*

*Door knockers and a tirling pin from town houses.*

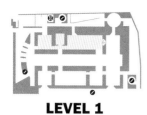

The regulation of manufacturing trades was done through craft guilds. A system of apprenticeship controlled a great range of craftsmen - bakers, butchers, skinners, candlemakers, smiths, weavers, tailors and many others. Material such as regalia and apprentice pieces tell us about how the guilds operated (Cases 16 and 17).

Many of the burghs were busy ports, exporting mainly raw materials and importing luxury goods and wine (Cases 9 and 10). Most of the trade was carried out with the Netherlands, the Baltic, Scandinavia and France. There are also displays exploring food and drink, from Scottish-made ale and whisky to wine imported from France and Germany (Cases 11, 12 and 13).

One inescapable feature of town life was the problem of supplying clean water and getting rid of waste. **Health and hygiene** (Case 14) shows material that illustrates the difficulties of keeping clean and the efforts to deal with the many diseases that were partly the consequence of poor hygiene.

Up the stairs you will find a focus on products made in Scotland, from everyday pottery (Case 20) to highly decorated pistols and swords (Case 19). **Scotland and Scandinavia** (Case 21) tells a fascinating story of imported timber used for a painted ceiling in Herdmanston House, East Lothian.

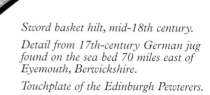

Go back down the stairs, past the panels from Mary of Guise's house, and turn right. This takes you into *The Medieval Church.*

*Sword basket hilt, mid-18th century.*

*Detail from 17th-century German jug found on the sea bed 70 miles east of Eyemouth, Berwickshire.*

*Touchplate of the Edinburgh Pewterers.*

# The Medieval Church

Christianity began to spread through Scotland in the fifth and sixth centuries AD. The story begins with *Early People* on Level 0. In *The Medieval Church* the focus is on life and belief after Christianity was established.

The first displays look at some of Scotland's early saints and pilgrimage, which both influenced Scottish religious life. We have already met St Andrew in *Scotland Defined*. The town of St Andrews was one of the most popular pilgrimage destinations within Scotland. Association with a saint or shrine often explains the survival of objects hundreds of years old. In Case 4 you can see three striking examples of this. The displays go on to examine the way the Church was organized and how it affected daily life. They continue downstairs, where the focus is on **The Church and the community**.

One of the most impressive objects linked with the Church in medieval Scotland is the crozier which belonged to Fillan, an eighth-century Irish saint who was active in Perthshire. Several relics of St Fillan have survived. The crozier left Scotland with an emigrant to Canada, but was returned some 60 years later and has ever since been in the care of the Museum (Case 14).

The Rotunda, back up the stairs, links *The Medieval Church* and *The Reformed Church*, through stonework and silver plate from James VII's chapel at Holyrood.

*Bell, 7th century, and bell shrine, 12th century, from Kilmichael Glassary, Argyll.*

*St Fillan's silver gilt crozier shrine.*

*Bronze figure of Christ found in Islay, Argyll, 13th century.*

Through the Rotunda you come to the start of *The Reformed Church*.

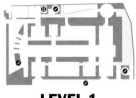

**LEVEL 1**

# The Reformed Church
## New ideas and forms of worship

In 1560 Scotland broke away from the Roman Catholic Church and adopted Protestantism. This, the Reformation, had a lasting impact on all aspects of life in Scotland. The form and language of church services were changed. The Bible and the new service books were in English and Scots rather than Latin, and people were encouraged to read them.

One of the first things you will notice in this gallery is a series of vividly painted wooden panels, the Dean panels. These are a reminder that the Reformation was part of the new thinking that produced the colour and vitality of the Renaissance.

Key aspects of the new forms of worship were communion and the centrality of the sermon. Now, the whole congregation shared in taking the bread and wine of the communion service, and communion cups and plates had to be large enough for general use. There are many examples of the new communion silver which illustrate this.

The Reformation was only the beginning of a long troubled period which saw fierce religious and political controversy. The second part of this gallery, **King and Covenant**, looks at the civil and religious wars of the Covenanters who resisted attempts to make the Scottish church conform with the English.

*Mask and wig of Covenanting minister Alexander Peden.*

*Book of Common Order in Scots, 1578.*

*Part of a painted panel from Dean House, Edinburgh.*

When you reach the end of the gallery, turn right into *New Horizons.*

34

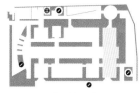

# New Horizons
## Scotland in the 17th century

*New Horizons* shows Scotland in a period of change. Although the 17th century saw conflict and disruption, it was also a time of new ideas and attitudes. Scotland was moving into a modern age.

The Huntly funeral procession displayed at the beginning of this theme illustrates medieval ideas of the importance of land and family. But times were changing, and you can explore some of the consequences through these displays. A new middle class began to rival traditional landowners in their homes and possessions, and often initiated new ideas. There was a flourishing cultural life. There is also evidence that women achieved more than is often suggested - look at the portrait of Esther Inglis, a successful professional woman.

New ideas were expressed in different ways. **From tower house to mansion house** shows how, with the passing of medieval family feuding, fortified houses gave way to more refined and decorated homes. Successful merchants and professional people could now adapt or build and furnish their new homes in fashionable styles which earlier only the nobility could have afforded.

Gardens were planned and laid out, often including an increasingly popular feature - a sundial. Several of these fascinating instruments, which reflect a growing interest in science and calculation, are displayed.

*Esther Inglis, calligrapher, 1595.*

*Lectern sundial with octagonal base.*

*Silver thistle cups, examples of fine 17th and 18th-century craftsmanship.*

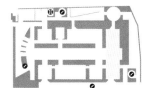

It was a creative and invigorating century for artists and craftworkers. Some of the work of silversmiths is shown in Cases 1 and 2. Scientists and intellectuals, merchants and politicians, also responded to the challenge of new ideas. Some of the advances in science are explored, with a particular emphasis on cartography - Scotland was one of the best mapped countries of the 17th-century world, thanks partly to the pioneering activities of Timothy Pont (Case 3). The process of mapping is examined in detail in a screen presentation.

But not everything was a success story. A keenness to benefit from trading opportunities in America and Africa led to the Darien scheme, an attempt to set up a Scottish colony in Central America (Case 4). Its failure was a bitter disappointment, and had political as well as economic consequences.

The end of the century intensified debate about the future of government in Scotland. Scotland's parliament had continued to meet in Edinburgh after the Union of the Crowns in 1603, making decisions on religious, economic and foreign policies. But just over 100 years after the country ceased to have a separate monarchy, the Scottish parliament ceased to exist (Case 5).

*The Riding of Parliament, probably the procession of 1685.*

*Lid of chest which held money and documents of the Company of Scotland.*

*Playing cards from a 17th-century pack showing the arms of nobles who sat in the Scottish parliament.*

To find out how this happened make your way by lift or stairs to Level 3, where *Scotland Transformed* begins with *The Union.*

# Scotland Transformed

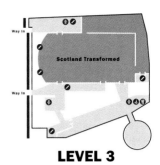

**LEVEL 3**

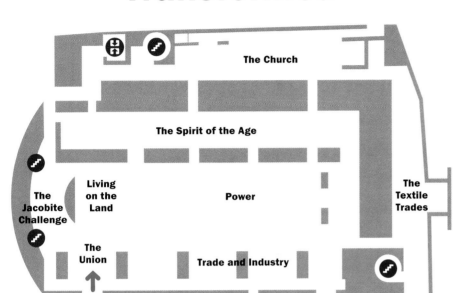

The Church

The Spirit of the Age

Living on the Land

The Jacobite Challenge

The Union

Power

Trade and Industry

The Textile Trades

The main entrance to *Scotland Transformed* on Level 3 takes you under the royal arms, an emblem of *The Union*.

In 1707 the parliaments of Scotland and England joined to form the parliament of the United Kingdom of Great Britain. On this level you will find some of the consequences of this change in the way Scotland was governed, which highlighted the process of transformation from a medieval to a modern society which had been going on throughout the previous century. In the central hall huge machines bear witness to part of that transformation - the Industrial Revolution.

With *Scotland Transformed* you are in the 18th and early 19th century. You can examine the Union itself, follow the fortunes of the Jacobite risings, and explore Scottish society at the time of the Enlightenment. You can look at the way the Church influenced both ordinary life and some of the period's major debates.

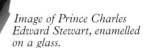

*Image of Prince Charles Edward Stewart, enamelled on a glass.*

*Detail from the silver gilt box presented to Henry Dundas by the burgh of Dumfries, 1793.*

*Snuff mulls and implements.*

*Weaving loom shuttles.*

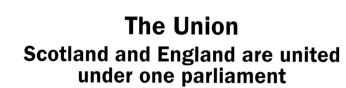

**LEVEL 3**

# The Union
## Scotland and England are united under one parliament

The Union of the parliaments has been a focus of debate ever since the beginning of the 18th century. The royal arms you pass under as you enter symbolize this new phase of British history. The consequences and repercussions of this change were felt in many areas of life in Scotland.

The display presents two key aspects of the Act of Union, beginning with the succession to the crowns and the setting up of a British parliament (Case 1). A main concern of the Act was to secure the throne for the Protestant faith, which excluded the exiled Catholic Stewarts and identified the Electress of Hanover as heir. Case 2 is about trade and the economy. The Act gave Scotland access to markets in England and her colonies overseas.

The objects displayed illustrate the relevant clauses of the treaty. Each clause was fiercely debated in the Scottish parliament, and the Scottish people also had strong views, expressed in the streets and in the press and pamphlets. Some of the key players in the debate are presented on the panel to the right as you go in.

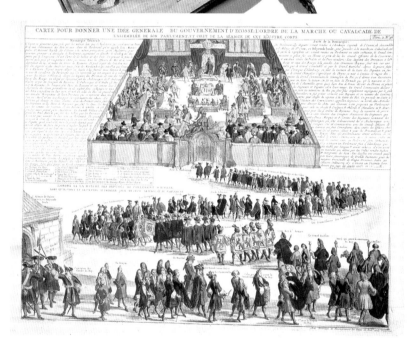

As you leave the *Union* a left turn takes you into *The Jacobite Challenge*, or turn right to look at themes dealing with Scotland's commerce and industry.

*Instrument of Authority confirming the storing of the Honours of Scotland in Edinburgh Castle.*

*Downsitting of Parliament, about 1680.*

*Silver medal of 1707, showing an intertwined rose and thistle.*

# Trade and Industry

Early in the 18th century many manufacturing trades were still carried on as they had been in the Middle Ages. This would soon change, though the pace of change was faster in the growing cities than in more rural areas.

New industries and new markets developed. Some, like linen manufacture (Case 3), were encouraged by the provisions of the Act of Union. In the first part of *Trade and Industry* you can see how Glasgow in particular benefited from the expansion of overseas trade. The tobacco and sugar trades were the foundations of the city's success (Case 2). Many other industries, such as glass and ceramics, were expanding at this time, particularly in the valleys of the Rivers Forth and Clyde (Case 4).

Coal and iron were the essential ingredients in the take-off of industrial manufacture which began in the 18th century. Coal had been mined and iron worked in Scotland for centuries. The displays show how the use of both expanded very quickly (Cases 6, 7 and 8). A remarkable object in the **Coal** display is the serf's collar (Case 6), a reminder that until 1799 some of Scotland's coal was mined by virtual slave labour.

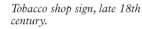

*Tobacco shop sign, late 18th century.*

*Arms of the Incorporated Trades of Dalkeith.*

*Collar of a serf who belonged to mineowner Sir John Erskine.*

The foundation of the Carron Ironworks in 1759 was a milestone in Scotland's industrial development. Soon Scotland became a world leader in the smelting and founding of iron. In the 19th century steel production opened up new possibilities.

Wrought and cast iron had a great range of industrial and domestic uses, from the carronade, perhaps the most famous product of the Carron Ironworks, to a cast iron teapot (Case 10). Later, with the development in 1856 of the Bessemer converter which enabled bulk steel making, steel came into the picture (Case 11). One of Scotland's most famous steel structures is the Forth Rail Bridge.

If coal was the fuel of the Industrial Revolution, money was also essential to make the wheels turn. Displays illustrate how Scotland took the lead in many aspects of banking and insurance, pioneering branch banking, the wide acceptance of banknotes and the overdraft (Cases 12 and 13).

Coal, iron and steel, money - all essential ingredients of Scotland's industrial revolution. As you've been looking at this theme the great machines in the centre of the hall have kept you company. They are part of *Power - from Water to Steam* which continues the story of Scotland's industrial development.

But we suggest that first you retrace your steps to the cruck house which is the main feature of *Living on the Land*.

*Cast iron umbrella stand made by the Callendar Iron Company, Falkirk, 1888.*

*Carronade, cannon made by the Carron Company, 1781.*

*Banknotes of the Union Bank of Scotland and the Royal Bank of Scotland.*

# Living on the Land

Life on the land changed more slowly than in the centres of industrial manufacture. In the country most people continued to depend on what they could produce themselves. The land provided not only food but the materials used for tools and domestic objects. In remoter parts of Scotland this was still the case in the early 20th century.

Dominating the *Living on the Land* display is a partly-reconstructed cruck-framed house. It comes from Dunbartonshire, and is typical of ordinary Lowland rural houses of the time. It illustrates some of the materials and techniques used in building. Inside the cruck house you can see the hearth, the focal point of domestic life, and objects typical of rural domestic life. Peat was the normal fuel of the fire.

Cased displays show the kinds of objects that were made for everyday use - creels and baskets, simple furniture and a variety of tools and utensils, all made from materials such as wood, plants, stone, and animal skins, bone and horn. One important domestic task was the spinning of home-produced wool into yarn. Beside the display of hand-spinning equipment there is a handloom which links rural activity with the machines in the hall beyond.

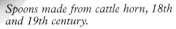

*Spoons made from cattle horn, 18th and 19th century.*

*Baskets, commonly used in rural areas in the 18th and 19th century.*

*Spearing salmon at night with a leister, early 19th century.*

The handloom marks the beginning of *Power - from water to steam,* which dramatically illustrates that while much of rural life changed only slowly, industry was in the process of a revolution.

# Power
## from water to steam

Water power had been used in manufacturing processes since the Middle Ages. The discovery that steam could drive machines transformed manufacturing and made the Industrial Revolution possible. *Power* tells the story of this transformation, particularly as it affected textile production. First spinning and then weaving moved from the home to the factory.

Steam technology began early in the 18th century, but a crucial development was James Watt's invention in 1769 of the separate condenser (Case 3). This and other improvements introduced by Watt led to efficient steam engines that were able to drive all kinds of machinery. They soon became the main source of industrial power.

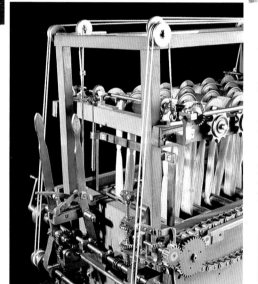

Displayed are engines, models and steam boilers which illustrate some of the stages that contributed to Scotland's industrial expansion (Cases 4 and 5). At the far end of the hall you can see models of some of the machines that were developed to produce and finish textiles (Cases 6, 7 and 8). The freestanding Corliss engine powered a small weaving mill in Alva, Clackmannanshire.

But the dominating machine here is the huge Newcomen atmospheric engine, a dramatic example of the power of steam. A rare survivor, it was used to pump water from coal mines near Kilmarnock, Ayrshire. An explanation of how it worked can be found in the screen presentation featured beside it.

*Power* began and finished with the manufacture of textiles. If you continue on into *The Textile Trades* you can find out more about Scotland's extraordinary achievement in making and selling textiles.

*The Newcomen pumping engine at Caprington Colliery, Kilmarnock, Ayrshire.*

*Model of a machine for dyeing hanks of wool.*

*Handloom from Kilbarchan, Renfrewshire.*

# The Textile Trades

In the first half of the 19th century textile manufacture played a vital part in the economy, with Scottish textiles sold throughout the world. Cotton became the main fabric manufactured in the west of Scotland. Tweeds and tartans made their contribution to high fashion, and for several decades there was a huge demand for shawls made in Paisley in a distinctive pattern that has ever since been identified with the town (Case 8). Dundee-made jute was used on every continent (Case 2). Less well known is the distinctive fabric made in the Vale of Leven (Case 5).

The handknitting tradition continued long after machine knitting had become common, and Shetland knitting along with the well-known Fair Isle pattern survived on a commercial basis (Case 6). But of all Scottish-made fabrics tartan is the best known, recognized throughout the world as an emblem of Scotland. It became fashionable in the 19th century, boosted by George IV's visit to Edinburgh in 1822. The king himself sported a tartan outfit. The climax of *The Textile Trades* is the display of tartan outfits worn for George IV's visit. Later, Queen Victoria's enthusiasm for Scotland and the royal family's taste for Highland dress further popularized tartan.

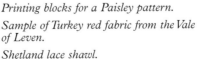

*Printing blocks for a Paisley pattern.*

*Sample of Turkey red fabric from the Vale of Leven.*

*Shetland lace shawl.*

*Suit in Mackintosh tartan, probably made for George IV's visit in 1822.*

The display of tartan links directly with *The Jacobite Challenge*. To find the start of this theme make your way back to *The Union* and turn left at the cruck house.

# The Jacobite Challenge

Here you will find the story of the Jacobite risings on behalf of the Stewarts who attempted to win back the crown from William and Mary and their successors the Hanovers.

The first attempt to reclaim the throne for the deposed James VII and II came in 1689, when Viscount Dundee's Jacobite army fought government troops at Killiecrankie (Case 1). Although they won the battle, Dundee was killed and the rising collapsed. For more than half a century the Jacobites, who took their name from Jacobus, the Latin for James, continued to try to win back the throne for the Stewart kings.

The displays look at the attempts at invasion by the Jacobites and some of the political consequences (Case 3). The final chapter came with the landing of Prince Charles Edward, James VII's grandson, on the west coast of Scotland in the summer of 1745. Bonnie Prince Charlie had grown up in exile and was hoping to regain the throne for his father James (Case 4). One of the most important objects associated with him is the silver travelling canteen which was recovered after his final defeat.

*Travelling canteen belonging to Prince Charles Edward Stewart.*

*Uniform of the Royal Company of Archers, which included many Jacobites.*

*Image of Prince Charles Edward.*

At first Charles Edward and his followers, drawn mainly from the Highland clans, were successful, taking Edinburgh and defeating General Cope at Prestonpans before continuing the march south into England. But Prince Charles was forced to give up his attempt to reach London, and with what was left of his army he returned to Scotland. The Duke of Cumberland led government troops in pursuit, finally catching up with the Jacobites on Culloden Moor near Inverness on 16 April 1746 (Case 5).

The Jacobite army was routed. Charles Edward was hunted by government troops but with the help of loyal followers escaped to France. Many of his supporters were less fortunate. Savage reprisals and government legislation pacified the Highlands once and for all (Case 7). Among the most poignant of the displayed relics of Culloden are two regimental colours which faced each other on the battlefield, those of the Jacobite Appin Stewarts and the government Barrell's Regiment.

Almost at once Bonnie Prince Charlie and the lost Jacobite cause were transformed into myth. Jewellery, portraits and personal items testify to the cult of relics that flourished for decades after the last hope of the Stewart kings had faded (Case 7).

*Sword and targe belonging to Prince Charles Edward Stewart.*

*Colours of Barrell's Regiment carried at Culloden.*

The end of the displays on the Jacobites takes you straight into the Riddles Court room, which begins *The Spirit of the Age.*

45

# The Spirit of the Age

'The spirit of the age,' said the great philosopher David Hume, 'affects all the arts' and spurs enquiry and improvement. He was talking about the Scottish Enlightenment of the 18th century, and the displays here look at the way people lived and thought at that time. They begin with a representation of a room from Riddles Court in Edinburgh's High Street, decorated with painted panels. In rooms like this notable Enlightenment figures gathered to debate and exchange ideas. David Hume himself lived for a while in Riddles Court.

The aspects of life in Enlightenment Scotland which follow are all linked: improvement, politics, architecture and town planning, education and the spread of ideas, social life and sports, the study and practice of medicine. Improvements in farming methods were found all over Scotland (Case 1). An example of an improved estate was Mellerstain in Berwickshire, where Lady Grisell Baillie ran a highly-organized home which reflected the benefits of changes on the land (Case 2).

Although there were advances in the arts, sciences and technology it was an uneasy time politically. **The State** (Cases 3 and 4) explores the political tensions that followed the Union and the Jacobite risings. The dominant player on Scotland's political stage at this time was Henry Dundas. You can see the freedom box presented to him by Dumfries.

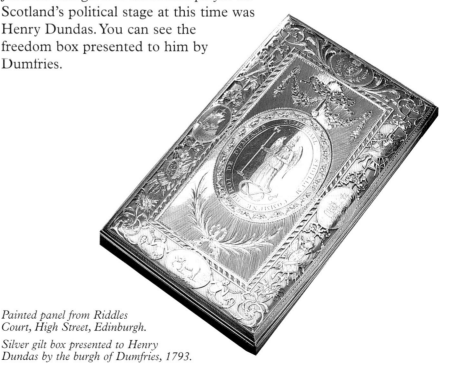

*Painted panel from Riddles Court, High Street, Edinburgh.*

*Silver gilt box presented to Henry Dundas by the burgh of Dumfries, 1793.*

An interest in the past influenced artists and architects as well as the antiquarians who enthusiastically collected and examined objects from earlier times (Case 5). Neo-classical architecture and town planning were among the results of the study of the classical world. Edinburgh's New Town is only one example.

Improved travel and communications were important factors in spreading new ideas (Case 6). More people were able to read and write, and so were better equipped to make the most of the new developments, both practical and intellectual. Many of these ideas were discussed in taverns and clubs, and at more polite gatherings to enjoy the newly fashionable beverage from China, tea (Case 7). There were plenty of opportunities for entertainment at all levels, whether at musical evenings or a day at the races, which attracted huge crowds (Cases 7 and 8).

Scotland had an international reputation for advances in science, particularly in medicine. Edinburgh's medical school was justly famous (Case 10). But in the mid-18th century medical learning probably affected only a tenth of Scotland's population, most of whom relied on traditional methods of dealing with ill health, illustrated by the charms and folk remedies in Case 9.

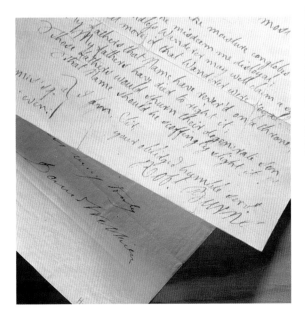

*Silver jack of the Edinburgh Society of Bowlers, 1771.*

*Silver mounted quaich, made from ebony and ivory, 18th century.*

*Letter from Robert Burns, 1788.*

Parallel to *The Spirit of the Age* is *The Church*. The best place to enter is across the bridge located between Cases 3 and 5.

**LEVEL 3**

# The Church

*Silver used in the communion service.*

In the 18th and 19th centuries most people belonged to the Church of Scotland, although both the Episcopal and Roman Catholic churches continued to have a role in Scottish religious life.

*The Church* focuses on some of the key aspects of worship and church government, beginning with the **Celebration of communion** (Cases 1A and 1B). The Church's social role is also explored. Membership of a church was initiated with baptism, and from that moment the kirk session had a role in judging and punishing the behaviour of individual members (Case 2). The gown and stool of repentance are striking reminders of the nature of public rebuke (Case 4). Parishes also made provision for the destitute and granted licences to beg, illustrated by the display of beggars' badges. Preaching continued to be central to Presbyterian worship. Sermons were often very long, timed by an hour glass (Case 3).

Disagreements about church government and how ministers were selected led to fierce debate and eventually to sections of the Church splitting off (Case 3). The most dramatic split came in 1843 with the Disruption of the Church of Scotland. About a third of the Church's ministers left to form the Free Church of Scotland. Later in the 19th century some sects reunited.

*Badges issued as licences to beg.*

You may like to continue the religious theme by going upstairs to *Daith Comes In* on Level 4. Also on Level 4 is *The Workshop of the World*. The stairs and lift are both at the east of this gallery.

# Daith Comes In

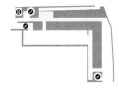

Scots were close to the realities of death in a society where disease, ill health or accident touched most families. This gallery looks at some of the rituals and customs surrounding death, burial and mourning.

The rituals of burial began in the home where the corpse remained while family and friends gathered to pay their respects (Case 1). There was usually a procession to the kirkyard with the coffin, either on foot or with a horse-drawn hearse. The hearse from Bolton, East Lothian, began to be used in the 1780s. The mortsafe is a reminder of the fear of grave robbers, who dug up corpses for the study of anatomy.

In Victorian times mourning customs became increasingly elaborate, with etiquette demanding not only the wearing of black clothes and jewellery but the use of a whole range of mourning accessories (Case 2). This could be costly - 'correct' mourning soon became a sign of status.

Older customs survived, and part of the display is concerned with some of the traditional beliefs that affected attitudes to death. Objects include charms and amulets, and the intriguing miniature coffins found on Arthur's Seat and never fully explained (Case 3).

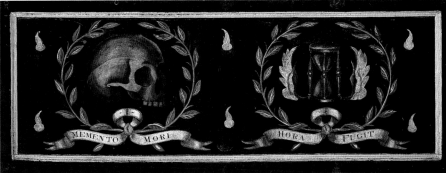

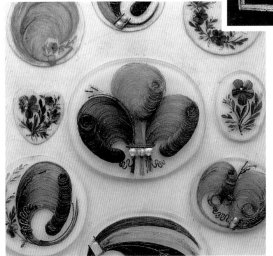

*Miniature coffins found on Arthur's Seat, Edinburgh.*

*Detail from a horse-drawn hearse from Bolton, East Lothian.*

*19th-century commemorative hair jewellery.*

If you make your way back to the Bolton hearse you can cross the bridge into the beginning of *The Workshop of the World*, which can also be entered direct from the stairs and lift at the east corner of the Museum.

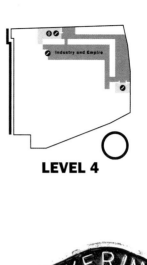

**LEVEL 4**

# Industry and Empire

Daith Comes In

Workshop of the World

Scottish life in the 19th century was shaped by industrial development and the consequences of exporting Scottish-made products all over the British Empire and to most other parts of the world.

Scotland rapidly became one of the most industrialized countries in Europe. From the factories, mills and shipyards came products ranging from ships and steam locomotives to fine fabrics and precision

*Maker's plate for Pickering & Co, engine builders.*

*Queens's Park Football Club badge.*

*Band of Courage Temperance Society Certificate, 1878.*

*Model of the express passenger locomotive* Waverley, *designed in 1906.*

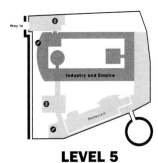

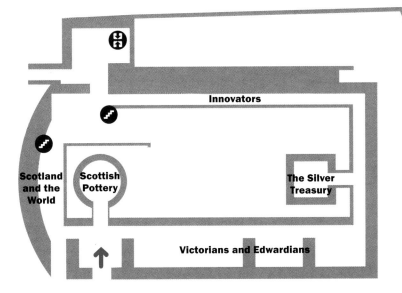

Innovators

Scottish
Pottery

Scotland
and the
World

The Silver
Treasury

Victorians and Edwardians

tools. Millions of people were a part of that process, through labour, initiative and tenacity. Many received its benefits, and were able to live healthier and more comfortable lives. But many more were victims of overcrowding and disease, also consequences of rapid industrialization.

*Industry and Empire* begins with *The Workshop of the World* on Level 4, where you can explore some of these industries. Upstairs on Level 5 the story continues, looking at some of their effects, especially on city life, and some of the ideas and issues that were important in Victorian and Edwardian society.

*Silver gilt workbox set with
'Scotch pebbles'.*

*Punch bowl made for George
Thomson, master of a whaling
ship, and Janet Thomson, 1825.*

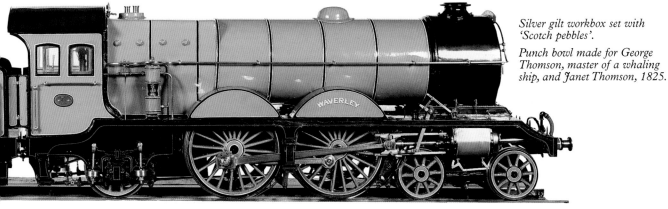

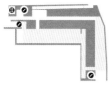

# The Workshop of the World

In the first part of *The Workshop of the World* you will find three crucial industries which carried the name of Scotland across the globe: railway engineering, whisky production and shipbuilding.

By the late 19th century Scotland was one of the world's major suppliers of railway equipment. As many as 58 companies built railway locomotives, with the main centres in Glasgow and Kilmarnock. Dominating the **Railway engineering** display is the steam locomotive *Ellesmere*, which was built in 1861 by Leith Engine Works, one of the smaller companies.

**Whisky distilling** has a long history in Scotland, but expanded as an industrial process in the 19th century (Case 4). It became an extremely valuable export and source of tax revenue. The essential ingredients of Scotland's distinctive malt whiskies are malted barley, water and the peat used to fuel the distilling process. The display looks at the process and the way the product was marketed, with pride of place taken by a copper wash still made to a traditional pattern for the Glenfiddich Distillery at Dufftown, Banffshire. A screen presentation explains the distilling process in more detail.

*Water jug advertising whisky made by Pattison's, an Edinburgh distiller.*

*Gold director's pass for Dundee, Perth and Aberdeen Railway, about 1850.*

*Steam locomotive* Ellesmere *at Bo'ness, built in Leith, 1861.*

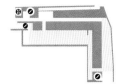
Of all Scotland's big industries **Shipbuilding** is perhaps the best known. In the 19th century the focus of Scotland's overseas trade shifted to the west coast, and the lower reaches of the River Clyde saw increasing activity in making ships. In the transition from wooden sailing ships to iron and steel steamships, Clyde builders and engineers were world leaders. Over the decades many hundreds of ships were built, from tugs and dredgers to huge passenger liners and warships. In 1867, 234 vessels were launched from 37 Clyde shipyards. The ship models displayed give a glimpse of some of this huge activity.

It wasn't enough to manufacture goods. Once built, they had to be transported to their destinations, which could be in Scotland or on the other side of the world. **By land and sea** looks at aspects of routes and transport and the all-important protection of shipping around Scotland's coasts. One of the most famous names in constructing and improving lighthouses and harbours is the Stevenson family of engineers. A great achievement of Robert Stevenson was the Bell Rock lighthouse, a model of which is featured in Case 11.

*The canal basin at Port Hopetoun, Edinburgh, illustrated on a punchbowl of about 1825.*

*Model of the SS* Nerbudda.

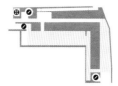

**LEVEL 4**

Roads, bridges, canals and railways all helped to open up the remoter parts of Scotland and speed up journeys. But there were setbacks. The collapse of the first Tay Bridge in a gale in December 1879 is also remembered, with a wrought iron girder that was found built into a house in Broughty Ferry on the Tay.

A huge range of other products played a part in Scotland's industrial success. **Made in Scotland**, which begins across the bridge at the end of **By land and sea**, looks at just a few of them. A lathe symbolizes engineering as the basis of industry. Printing and paper making developed rapidly in the 18th and 19th century, servicing a flourishing publishing industry (Cases 4 and 5). A printing press exhibited at the Great Exhibition in 1851 and used by Nelson's, the Edinburgh publishers, is displayed.

Scotland's chemical industry was stimulated by the needs of textile making, but a distinctive feature from the mid-nineteenth century was the production of shale oil (Case 6). This followed from the work of James 'Paraffin' Young. Another important industry, glassmaking, is explored in Case 7. Heavy ceramics - bricks, tiles, drainpipes and sanitary fittings - were needed to supply building work and the improvements to sanitation which were so important a feature of Victorian urban development (Case 8).

*The first rotary printing press, invented by Thomas Nelson, Edinburgh, 1850.*

*Detail from an illustration of Holyrood Glass Works, about 1910.*

*Industry and Empire* continues on Level 5.

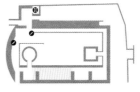

# Victorians and Edwardians
## The Effects of Industry

Provision for the needs of the huge numbers of people who came to live in towns and cities was a key Victorian issue. *The Effects of Industry* looks at some of the problems that arose, how they were tackled, and how life, particularly in the cities, was changing. It begins by looking at the contrast between the popular image of a romantic Highland Scotland and some of the realities of Victorian urban life (Cases 1 and 2).

City authorities gradually became aware of the need to deal with slum conditions. The provision of clean water and underground sewers was crucial to improving health (Case 2). Religious belief was a driving force in the reform movement, as well as a source of support for the underprivileged. Drunkenness was one of the many serious problems tackled, with the temperance movement making an impact, although it failed to transform drinking habits (Case 3). Another focus of Victorian energies was education. The Education Act of 1872 required all children between the ages of five and thirteen to go to school (Case 3).

Home and family were regarded as essential to social stability. The home was still the focus of most ceremonies marking birth, marriage and death, but, particularly for women, was also a workplace. Housework remained almost entirely the province of women, in their own homes or working as servants for others (Case 4).

*Pottery figures of a piper and a Highlander, early 19th century.*

*Plumbers Association badge marking the Reform Act of 1884.*

*Box of Britannia slate pencils.*

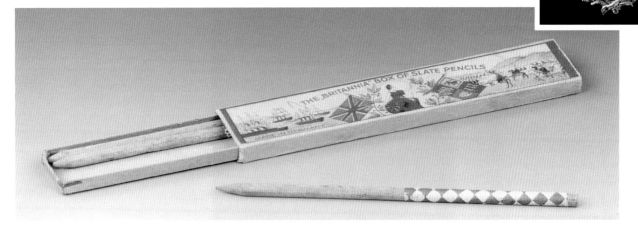

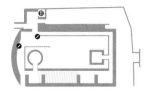

The freestanding displays of kitchen and laundry equipment show how the domestic environment was changing. The model of a household plumbing system illustrates how piped water could transform life - although only the middle classes could afford the benefits of these advances.

Working people were encouraged to help themselves, and many took steps to improve their lives and prospects (Case 6). Government legislation gradually shortened working hours and provided for holidays. The displays here illustrate some of the ways in which people made use of new-found leisure. Societies were formed and free libraries and museums were opened. Musical entertainment flourished. A display of holiday souvenirs (Case 6) reflects how, by the end of the century, more and more people had opportunities for trips and holidays as well as sports and games (Case 5). Golf became accessible to many more people, including women, and enthusiasm for football took off, with the first crowd of 100,000 watching a match in 1886.

All the displays in this area illustrate the explosion in the quantities of goods that were on sale. Factory production and improved transport, especially the coming of the railways, brought a huge range of products to centres of population, while advertising promoted them (Case 7).

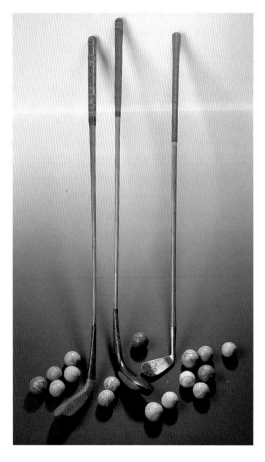

The gallery continues with *Victorians and Edwardians - the Rewards of Industry* which displays some of the huge range of consumer products which became available.

*Cast iron cooking pots.*

*Sheet music cover for 'The soldier's dream'.*

*Golf clubs and gutta-percha golf balls, late 19th century.*

# Victorians and Edwardians
## The Rewards of Industry

People had more money in their pockets and consumer spending took off. Two features vividly illustrate the new consumer society. The Great Exhibition held in London in 1851 was the first of many hugely popular international trade exhibitions to which people flocked in their thousands. Several international exhibitions were subsequently held in Glasgow and Edinburgh (Case 1).

Keeping pace with the popularity of these exhibitions was the growth of the department store, which encouraged customers to browse and choose from a great array of goods. The second part of this area is set up to suggest a typical Victorian department store.

First you come to the **Pottery and glass department** which displays a great variety of wares, from a ceramic hatpin holder to artistic glassware (Case 2). The **Silver and jewellery department** supplied discerning and wealthy customers with domestic silver and fashionable jewellery, much of it set with the Scottish semi-precious stones - pebble jewellery - which were so popular at the time (Case 4).

A late 19th-century novelty was the gramophone, which revolutionized music in the home (Case 3). The washstand with its Wemyss Ware toilet set being admired by a woman and her small son is typical of what could be purchased to furnish a tasteful and opulent home (Case 5).

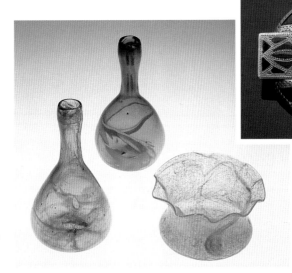

*Senior Monarch gramophone, early 20th century.*

*Circular silver brooch set with red and green polished stones, a design registered in 1875.*

*Examples of Clutha glass made in the City Glass Works, Glasgow, late 19th century.*

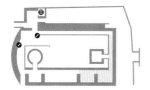

## LEVEL 5

Much of what department stores offered for sale was mass-produced and relatively inexpensive. Those who could afford something more exclusive could commission work from the many innovative artists and designers who were making names for themselves. Charles Rennie Mackintosh and Sir Robert Lorimer are two of the best known, but women were playing an increasingly important part in Scotland's artistic life. Part of the display on commissioning is devoted to the work of Phoebe Traquair, Jessie M King and others. Phoebe Traquair, who lived and worked in Edinburgh, is represented by jewellery and bookbindings (Case 8). The range and vitality of some of the leading Glasgow-based women artists is shown in Case 9.

Charles Rennie Mackintosh became known through his designs for the tearooms opened by Kate Cranston at the turn of the century. You will find several examples of furniture and decoration from Glasgow's tearooms, designed by Mackintosh and others. The close relationship between Lorimer and the decorative metalwork firm of Thomas Hadden is explored through a display of wrought iron work (Case 7).

Lorimer developed the design for the **Scottish National War Memorial**, devised to commemorate the loss of life in the First World War and completed in 1927. Lorimer recruited Edinburgh men and women to work on the Memorial (Case 9).

Opposite the Earlshall gates is the entrance to *The Silver Treasury* which presents a changing display of Scottish silver. If you continue to the end of *The Rewards of Industry* and turn left, you enter *Innovators*.

*Hairbrush and mirror set designed by Jessie M King, 1911.*

*Embossed leather bookbinding by Phoebe Traquair.*

*Mantel clock made by Marion Wilson, about 1900.*

# The Silver Treasury

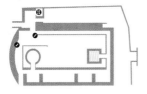

Scotland's tradition of craftsmanship in silver and gold goes back to prehistory, and you will find examples of Scottish silver throughout the Museum. *The Silver Treasury* presents a more detailed look at how that tradition developed and how the craft was organized from the 16th century.

It is not possible to identify individual makers before the middle of the 16th century, but after that time makers' marks enable much more to be known about craftsmen and where they worked. You will find examples of silver from all over Scotland, from the 16th century to the present day. The display includes pieces commissioned by the Museum from contemporary silversmiths working in Scotland.

The displays change on a regular basis, in order to allow visitors to see as much as possible from the Museum's collection, but they always feature different types of silver, ranging from cutlery to tea services, including pieces such as quaichs, thistle cups and the striking egg-shaped urns which are uniquely Scottish.

Although Edinburgh was always the main centre, many other Scottish towns produced notable and attractive silverware, and a section on **Burgh silver** presents examples from several of them.

*Silver and enamel vase by Maureen Edgar, 1989.*

*Casket made in 1894 for the 1st Marquis of Breadalbane.*

*Urn, tray and bullet-shaped tea pot by James Ker, 1730s.*

Turn left as you exit from *The Silver Treasury* and left again at the end of *The Rewards of Industry* to find the start of *Innovators.*

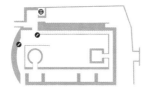

# Innovators

Evidence of the way Scots have made their mark in many different fields can be found all over the Museum. *Innovators* draws together some of the most distinguished Scots of the 18th and 19th centuries to explore in more depth their contributions in the fields of science and technology, exploration and travel, politics and the arts. The displays will change to feature different individuals.

Scots have been in the forefront of mapping and opening up territories in North America, Africa and Australasia: John Rae in the Canadian Arctic and David Livingstone in southern Africa are just two examples. Scotland's landscape has been attracting geologists for several hundred years, and it's not surprising that in the sciences Scotland's own geologists have made a particular impact. Two of the most innovative were James Hutton and Hugh Miller. We have selected only a few of the dozens of Scots who have made a name in technological development and invention. And we feature Scotland's three best-known writers: Burns, Scott and Stevenson, each of whom developed a unique voice and has been hugely influential around the world.

You can find out more about individuals and topics featured in *Innovators* in other parts of the Museum of Scotland and in the Royal Museum next door.

Continue to the beginning of *Scotland and the World*, which you can also enter from the southeast lift and stairs from Level 4.

*Statue of Hugh Miller, geologist, writer and lay theologian, 1802-56.*

*Medal commemorating David Livingstone, missionary and explorer, 1813-73.*

*Model of the pioneering steamboat* Charlotte Dundas, *designed by William Symington, 1803.*

# Scotland and the World

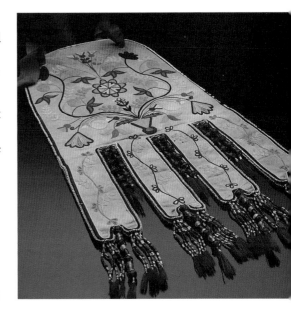

Although Scots had always travelled widely and lived and worked abroad, in the 18th and 19th centuries much larger numbers settled permanently overseas. The world map which introduces this theme traces Scottish placenames all over the world, and suggests just how much of a mark Scots have made.

They left Scotland for many reasons, to seek new opportunities, out of a sense of adventure or duty, often because they were forced to leave their homes (Case 1). North America attracted Scots from the early days of British colonization. By the late 18th century more than 150,000 Scots had settled there (Case 2). The rate of emigration increased in the 19th century, when Australia and New Zealand were also attracting emigrants. Scots in Africa and India made an impact as missionaries, soldiers, administrators and traders (Case 3).

The material displayed sheds a fascinating light on Scots abroad. There is a Gaelic Bible which travelled to North Carolina (Case 2), a deerskin bag designed and used by John Rae who explored and mapped Arctic Canada (Case 2), wallpaper inspired by the South African War, featuring Scottish regiments (Case 3), and the tea clipper *Cutty Sark*, a symbol of Scottish enterprise in the Far East (Case 3).

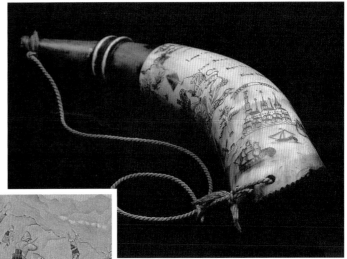

*Scotland and the World* also looks at men and women on the move within Scotland, and Irish immigration (Case 4).

*Deerskin bag belonging to John Rae, Arctic explorer.*

*Powder horn engraved with a map of northeast America, used in the French and Indian wars, 1754-63.*

*Wallpaper with scenes of the South African War, 1899-1902.*

If you began your visit to Level 5 at the start of *Victorians and Edwardians*, you have now come full circle. The entrance to *Scottish Pottery* is directly opposite the main entrance to this floor.

61

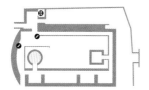

# Scottish Pottery

Throughout the Museum you can see pottery, much of it made in Scotland, some from overseas. In the middle of the 18th century pottery began to be made in Scotland on an industrial scale.

Scotland's potteries grew up in the Forth and Clyde valleys, where there were local supplies of clay, and more importantly of coal which fuelled the kilns. A model kiln is a key feature of the display. The first industrial pottery was Delftfield in Glasgow, set up in 1748. Other firms soon followed and by the next century there were several large potteries in the Glasgow area with successful overseas trade (Case 2). In 1750 a large-scale pottery was set up in Prestonpans, East Lothian, the first of several in the area (Case 1). Like the west-coast potteries, the Forth valley firms produced a range of earthenware and porcelain items.

The display includes some of the most distinctive Scottish products, including the oriental-patterned plates and bowls produced by J & M P Bell for export to southeast Asia (Case 2) and the well-known Wemyss Ware from Kirkcaldy(Case 4). The material will be regularly changed, to allow visitors to see as much as possible of the Museum's very rich collection of Scottish pottery.

*Plate made by J & M P Bell & Co Ltd, Glasgow, for export to southeast Asia.*

*Porcelain jug made in 1827 by Reid's of Musselburgh for Robert Moffat, a market gardener of Fordeldean, Midlothian.*

*Wemyss Ware plate made by Heron's Fife Pottery.*

*One of the Over Hailes porcelain mugs made by William Littler's West Pans factory, about 1770.*

Displays continue on Level 6 with *Twentieth Century*, which can be reached by stairs or lift.

# Twentieth Century

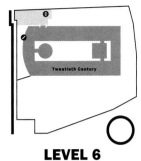

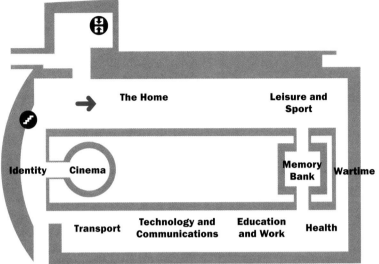

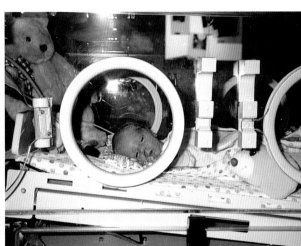

Where can you find Oor Wullie, Doc Martens boots, Irn Bru and a Bible with a bullet hole? Where can you see the Queen Mother's tartan sash and hear Queen's 'Bohemian Rhapsody'? Toast, televisions, tubeless tyres and teddy bears - what's the connection? *Twentieth Century* is where the answers are.

Here, we have asked the people of Scotland to decide what should be displayed. Distinguished individuals and the general public were invited to nominate objects which in their view made a significant impact on 20th-century life in Scotland, or which had a personal story to tell. Out of all the suggestions made, over 300 items - including those above - have been selected.

Washing machines and biro pens have affected the lives of most of us, but many of the objects have a very personal meaning - for example, an organ donor card and a grandmother's perfume. The material is divided into areas covering aspects of life at home and at work, at war and at leisure. You will find not only the objects themselves, but also the contributors' reasons for suggesting them.

*Harris Davidson in the incubator which saved his life when he was born prematurely. Chosen by Janice Davidson, his mother.*

*Smudge, the People's Palace cat, and replicas made to raise money to buy a computer for this Glasgow museum. Chosen by Elspeth King.*

63

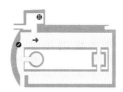

**LEVEL 6**

The exhibition is a mosaic of individual lives and the things that have been important in them. It expresses feelings about war and loss as well as about new opportunities. It reflects enormous change - in working and domestic life, in leisure, in health, and in the way we communicate. Many of these changes are shared with other nations; others are part of a very Scottish story.

In the Memory Bank you can find out more about the contributors and the whole range of suggestions made. Here you have an opportunity to make your own contribution by adding your choice of objects to represent Scotland in the 20th century.

One feature of the 20th century which has probably touched the life of every Scot is the moving picture, and *Twentieth Century* includes a small cinema with seats from the 1930s, the heyday of film-going and also of Scottish documentary film making. The cinema shows archive documentaries and other short films.

And for a wider picture continue up to the roof garden. You will get a spectacular view of Edinburgh and the surrounding countryside, from the Pentland Hills to Fife beyond the Firth of Forth. It embraces a great deal of what you have been looking at in the Museum - the making of the landscape, early settlement, commerce and conflict, religion, learning and creativity, diplomacy and domestic life. It is both Scotland in the present and millions of years of Scotland in the past.